I0459143

Endorsements

"I've been in ministry for 55 years, and for 53 of those I've been married to a biology teacher. Faith and science, like our marriage, are beautifully intertwined for those who want to understand God more completely. Mr. Wong has written a remarkable book—winsome, concise, and compelling—that explores the likelihood of God as Creator, the reliability of Scripture, and the reality of Jesus. His writing invites readers on an exciting adventure where honest questioning, both in faith and in science, leads to 'aha!' moments of discovery and a deeper confidence in God. This is one book every seeker—and every believer—should read for a stronger, more contagious faith."

Rev. Dr. Joel C. Hunter
Pastor of Community Benefit, Action Church and
Chairman, Central Florida Pledge

"Evan approaches complex questions of faith with grace and clarity. His ability to write with clear and relatable communication makes this book an accessible and insightful resource for anyone seeking guidance and understanding on spiritual matters."

Pastor Tyler Althof
CCO, Action Church, Maitland, FL

"Evan Wong doesn't try to convince the reader to believe in anything in particular. Instead, he aims to clear any preconceived biases one might have against Christianity and show that certain things that we deem "unbelievable" are in fact not as out of the realm of possibility as we thought. Even if you aren't moved to begin your journey into faith, this is a book that will help you become more open-minded and less judgmental."

Mitchell Wiginton, Agnostic

"This book is a short but powerful read that helps the reader think deeper about God and Christianity. It connects science, history, and reason in a way that strengthens belief and invites honest reflection."

Pastor Eddie Rivera
Senior Associate Pastor, Action Church, Maitland, FL

"*Faith Isn't Blind* is a refreshing and thoughtful guide for anyone wrestling with questions about God, truth, or belief. Evan doesn't shy away from the hard questions, but he also doesn't let skepticism have the final word. This book will challenge your mind, strengthen your faith, and remind you that doubt isn't the enemy of belief, but it's often the pathway to it."

Pastor Nick Drake
Pastor, Action Church, Sanford, FL

Faith Isn't Blind

A SHORT GUIDE FOR
THE SKEPTICAL, THE SEARCHING,
AND THE OPEN-MINDED

Evan Wong

HigherLife Publishing

OVIEDO, FLORIDA

HigherLife Development Services, Inc.
2342 Westminster Terrace, Oviedo, FL 32765
(407) 563-4806, HigherLifePublishing.com

© 2025 by Evan Wong

All rights reserved. No part of this book may be reproduced without written permission from the publisher or copyright holder, nor may any part of this book be transmitted in any form or by any means electronic, mechanical, photocopying, recording, or other, without prior written permission from the publisher or copyright holder.

Scripture quotations marked "NIV" are taken from the Holy Bible, New International Version®, NIV®. Copyright © 1973, 1978, 1984, 2011 by Biblica, Inc.™ Used by permission. All rights reserved worldwide.

Scripture quotations marked "ESV" are from the ESV® Bible (The Holy Bible, English Standard Version®), copyright © 2001 by Crossway, a publishing ministry of Good News Publishers. Used by permission. All rights reserved.

Published 2025
Printed in the United States of America

30 29 28 27 26 25   1 2 3 4 5

ISBN: 978-1-964081-66-3 (paperback)
ISBN: 978-1-964081-67-0 (ebook)
Copyright Case Number: 1-14979089461

Dedication

For my incredible sister, Marissa, my inspiration for writing this book. May you find some answers in these pages.

Thank you to my beautiful wife, Camryn—my biggest supporter and my perfect proof of God's existence. I love you so very much.

Epigraph

*"Now faith is confidence in what we hope for
and assurance about what we do not see."*
Hebrews 11:1 (NIV)

*"Your word is a lamp to my feet
and a light to my path."*
Psalm 119:105 (ESV)

Contents

Acknowledgments

Thank you to the family at HigherLife Publishing. Thank you, Dave Welday, for giving me a path forward during a time of confusion. You encouraged and inspired me to move forward with this opportunity, and I would not be at this point if it weren't for you and your incredible team.

A special thank you to my manager, Faithe Stephens, and editors, Esse Johnson, Libbye Morris, and Ashley Niro. You all helped me create something even greater than I could've ever imagined. I am thankful to share this journey with you all, and I pray we are able to bring many people to Christ through all our effort. God bless you all!

To my readers, I pray you all find some answer and security throughout this book. If it had an impact on your life, I pray that you would share what you have learned and make disciples of all nations. Lord, we ask that You bring wisdom and peace to all those who ask—that You soften the hearts of those who are yet to experience Your love.

PART 1

Science Does Not Oppose Faith

Are you a reasonable person?

Most of us like to think we are. We all hold opinions, and it's good to have a stance on important topics. But what about the controversial ones? Are you open to hearing someone else's opinion, even when you're emotionally invested in your own?

It's good to follow evidence to a given conclusion, no? Yet what happens when the evidence brings us almost to the end—but not directly to a conclusion? In those moments, we ultimately have to make a decision based on where the evidence is leading and commit to a conclusion with an educated guess.

The struggle with faith is no different.

You've probably heard the phrase "blind faith." It refers to believing in something without proof, evidence, or reason, and trusting in that belief, even if it seems unreasonable or there is evidence to the contrary. Sometimes people say Christians abide by "blind faith" because we believe in Jesus Christ, even though we've never personally *seen Him*.

I would argue that *faith isn't blind.* On the contrary—our faith is based on evidence that Jesus existed and impacted people in unprecedented ways. True faith isn't merely irrational belief without evidence. Instead, it is active, reasoned, and supported by transformed lives and historical evidence.

Four Groups of People

There are four groups of people, and their personal belief systems can be summed up like this:

1. I fully reject any belief in a God, and nothing can be said or done that would convince me otherwise.
2. I don't think there is a God, but if there were sufficient scientific or historical evidence, I would consider the claims.
3. I believe in God due to scientific, historical, and personal evidence. However, if there were compelling evidence against it, I would not have—nor would I have ever come to—my belief.
4. I fully believe in God, and nothing can be said or done that could change my mind.

Which belief resonates with you the most?

If you answered 1 or 4, you might as well stop reading. Your mind is made up, and nothing that's said or done could change your worldview.

Those with a 1 mindset often have an emotional investment against any form of faith. It's not a *head* issue; it's a *heart* issue. For one reason or another, they don't want it to be true, so they won't listen to the evidence. The 4s are committed to their belief, and nothing can change their minds.

The 2s and 3s are the intellectually honest ones—and I believe that's where most people fall. They have the humility to consider opposing beliefs, even if those beliefs don't end up changing their own. Whether raised in faith, atheism, or something else entirely, they've taken an educated step toward where they stand today. No matter what your upbringing was like, at some point you either affirmed it—or ran from it.

Intellectual Commitments

Richard Lewontin, an atheist geneticist, wrote the following:

> Our willingness to accept scientific claims that are against common sense is the key to an understanding of the real struggle between science and the supernatural. We take the side of science *in spite* of the patent absurdity of some of its constructs … *in spite* of the tolerance of the scientific community for unsubstantiated just-so stories, because we have a prior commitment … to materialism.

> It is not that the methods and institutions of science somehow compel us to accept a material explanation of the phenomenal world, but, on the contrary, that we are forced by our *a priori* adherence to material causes to create an apparatus of investigation and a set of concepts that produce material explanations, no matter how counterintuitive, no matter how mystifying to the uninitiated. Moreover, that materialism is absolute, for we cannot allow a Divine Foot in the door.[1]

Does that sound reasonable? To reject any evidence that leads anywhere other than materialism? That's the stance of a lot of the 1s. They commit themselves to materialism, trapping themselves in a fixed hallway of closed doors, forcing science to fit only where they say it should go. Lewontin essentially admits here that without a precommitment to materialism, much of the evidence would seem quite absurd—and would actually contradict his worldview.

My objective here is to advocate for the position of the 3s. I hope the 2s have the humility to listen and consider why being a 3 is not unreasonable, especially from a Christian perspective. Many people fall away from faith— or they reject it as a whole—because they believe all religion is just a simple fairytale explanation of the universe. But that's not the case. Many believers have doubt. Un-

---

1   Richard Lewontin, "Billions and Billions of Demons," in a review of *The Demon-Haunted World: Science as a Candle in the Dark* by Carl Sagan (The New York Review of Books, January 9, 1997), 31.

fortunately, they're sometimes told they *can't* doubt, when in reality, the very nature of doubt is what leads people to search for—and find—evidence for their faith.

> It is no good asking for a simple religion. After all, real things are not simple…. Reality, in fact, is usually something you could not have guessed. That is one of the reasons I believe Christianity. It is a religion you could not have guessed. If it offered us just the kind of universe we had always expected, I should feel we were making it up.[2]

Many nonbelievers, on the other hand, see the claims of science as ultimate truth that should be taken at face value. This is a mistake because of the inconsistency of science. Our knowledge of the world and our universe is constantly changing, and there is no sign that we truly know anything with certainty.

If we clung to our worldview and never deviated from it, would we not still believe that the sun and planets revolve around the earth? Should we not be afraid of sailing too close to the edge of the earth? No—because science has revealed that these beliefs are not true. Science helps us get closer to the truth, but scientists (the interpreters) get things wrong, and their conclusions don't make the thing true in themselves. We make some progress, but every new discovery just reveals how much we do not know.

---

2   C. S. Lewis, *Mere Christianity* (HarperOne, 2009), 41.

> Science is constantly changing, developing, standing in need of correction, although (we trust) becoming more and more accurate. If the biblical explanation were at the level, say, of the twenty-second-century science, it would likely be unintelligible to most people, maybe even including scientists today.[3]

Now, this is not to say that science cannot be trusted. Faith in God is highly compatible with science. When taking an honest approach to scientific discoveries, we find Christians don't have many objections. Most objections come down to interpretation.

Christians need to know that we are not trying to win arguments. If our understanding or interpretations on certain topics are not requirements for salvation, then we do not need to risk turning people away from faith because of an opinion—especially because it's not essential to the core of Christianity. If our opinions are dissuading people from considering Christianity, then we are missing the point.

Within our own community, Christians disagree on a lot, so a difference in interpretation on noncritical issues shouldn't keep anyone from exploring faith. If there is wide disagreement on an issue, we can hold a position while also understanding that it may be a faulty interpretation of information.[4]

---

3   John Lennox, *Seven Days That Divide The World, 10th Anniversary Edition: The Beginning According to Genesis and Science* (Zondervan Reflective, 2021), 26.

4   Ibid., 30–31.

My goal is not to *force faith* on anyone. Nor is my goal to disprove science or to bend science to fit Christianity. The objective here is to at least show that we need to expect our understanding of the universe to be flexible. It is to show that there are always alternative views, regardless of the subject. A Christian can be wrong about something in science, but that doesn't make the Bible false, just as discoveries that align with the Bible don't automatically make the Bible true. My goal is simply to show that we don't know as much as we think we do and that there are other logical interpretations worth considering.

Some think that Christians are a bunch of crazy people, but that's often because we grow up being told that Christianity and science are incompatible. Everyone believes that the opposing side "just doesn't get it." It is our worldviews that cause distaste for the other side and automatically lead us to reject any claim offered by our opposition that challenges our interpretations.

If science "does not leave room for Christianity," then why do we see that 65.4 percent of Nobel Prize Laureates from 1901 to 2000 identified as Christian? The statistics show that science does not oppose faith. Both theistic and atheistic scientists have a worldview and are making a truth claim about our universe.[5]

The atheist assumes there is no God and uses that logic in an effort to prove that there is no need for God. Assuming a theory to be fact is a slippery slope to bad science.

5   John C. Lennox, *Can Science Explain Everything?* (The Good Book Company, 2024), 17.

We need to be careful not to allow emotions to lead us toward the conclusion we want.

Belief in the Unreasonable

Everyone believes in something unbelievable. Theists believe in God, whom they cannot directly see or prove, and atheists search for any evidence that they cannot see or prove in order to disprove God.

You may say, "Oh, I don't need faith; I have confidence in science." The issue is that *nonbelief* is a belief system. It's a worldview you're trying to adhere to—one in which you place your confidence.

The Christian worldview works the same way. It's still a belief system, but we believe that framework begins with a mind behind it all. You may be thinking that the word *faith* discounts anything I'm saying here. However, you would still have *confidence* that your worldview is correct. The word *confidence* stems from the Latin *con fide*—literally meaning *with faith*.

We're not all that different. Your *confidence* and my *faith* are the same thing.

Lack of faith is ultimately a decision, not a conclusion. The door for God is wide open, and it is one that science will never close. You can decide to live your life as if the door is closed and try to make everything fit into the room you're in, but is that reasonable? Are you staying in the room because of your emotions or because you "have confidence in science"? You could also take a look outside and see if things still make sense.

The atheist or materialist worldview is just as—if not more—difficult to comprehend. People are raised to believe that because we have science, we don't need God. But as we've discussed, these two things are not exclusive.

I'm not using God to explain what science can explain on its own. The further we advance in science, the more incredible this universe becomes—and science reveals a universe that couldn't have come to be by random chance.

The bottom line is that if there is historical evidence and scientific plausibility that someone named Jesus walked this earth, died, and rose again—then we should listen to what His claims were. And if we believe He lived, died, and rose again, then it is not because of "blind faith" but because of evidence of His resurrection.

I understand that "rising from the dead" is a bit of a stretch for most people. Miracles, in general, tend to be the hang-up. People have preconceived notions about miracles, so we'll start there.

PART 2

Miracles

Miracles were always my biggest hang-up when it came to believing in Christianity. The word itself can feel heavy and loaded with assumptions, which is why so many of us struggle with it. But the truth is, miracles do exist—and, in one way or another, we all believe they happen.

A miracle is generally understood to be an extraordinary or highly improbable event that results in unusually positive or welcome outcomes.

That's not far off from how we describe anomalies or phenomena. How would you define these? They're events for which the cause and outcome are both in question. They tend to defy the scientific laws as we know them. Any time the word *miracle* is used, the word *anomaly* or *phenomenon* could take its place. Christians may use the word *miracle* more loosely than we should, but that doesn't take away from the fact that a miracle is simply a deviation from what normally occurs.

The objection here might be that scientific laws can't be broken—that we just haven't found the explanation for the anomalies or phenomena we observe. However, what exactly is a law?

A law is something we as humans have observed and deemed to be true. However, if the universe is as old as it's believed to be, then is it not possible that the laws are just what is usually true—and not *absolutely* true?

Remember what we discussed earlier about how scientific views are constantly changing and becoming more complex? Our laws help guide us in the correct direction when trying to make scientific advancements, but we need to follow evidence where it leads. We assume the laws are constant to uphold science, but there's still the possibility of error in our understanding of any given law.

> The principle of following evidence where it leads is extremely important. It may mean that we have to go beyond narrowly defined scientific explanations in terms of natural processes, but it need not lead us beyond rational explanation. It might even lead us to the right explanation![6]

There's no reason to believe the laws of nature are stable and constant—unless there is a *Legislator* keeping them that way. We expect to see the laws—and order—in nature because we believe these laws were calculated and given to us. The constants in our universe—like gravity and the expansion rate—are far too precise to be left to chance. Even if they had come about randomly, it would

---

6   Ibid., 61.

be difficult to believe they've remained this stable over time without a governing force to guide it. "When a miracle takes place, it is the laws of nature that alert us to the fact that it is a miracle."[7]

Just because something is outside what we call "the law" doesn't mean it can't happen. It's the laws that draw our attention to the anomaly—the thing that doesn't fit with what we've observed over time. Our observations— what we call "laws"—aren't closed just because we say so. We've had only a few hundred, maybe a few thousand years, to observe and define them. It's still our assumption—and often our educated guess—that they're consistent. The laws may be immutable, but it's equally plausible that we haven't yet gotten everything right.

For instance, it's rather bold to claim that the laws of nature are absolute—and bolder still to assume they'll remain the same, even though we've seen neither the past nor the future.

You could claim that there are no diamonds in Florida because you've never found any there. But to prove that there are indeed no diamonds, you'd have to search every square inch—down to the earth's core. All it takes is one speck to prove your assertion false.

The same applies to our observations of the laws of nature. We can name laws according to our observations, but we must understand that the door might yet be open; we could still discover something entirely unexpected. The beauty and advancement of science lie in the changes

---

7   Ibid., 81.

that come from new discoveries, not in clinging to a narrow view of the universe.

> If you take a thing like a stone or a tree, it is what it is and there seems no sense in saying it ought to have been otherwise. Of course you may say a stone is "the wrong shape" if you want to use it for a rockery, or that a tree is a bad tree because it does not give you as much shade as you expected. But all you mean is that the stone or the tree does not happen to be convenient for some purpose of your own. You are not, except as a joke, blaming them for that. You really know, that, given the weather and the soil, the tree could not have been any different. What we, from our point of view, call a "bad" tree is obeying the laws of its nature just as much as a "good" one....
>
> It follows that what we usually call the laws of nature—the way weather works on a tree, for example—may not really be laws in the strict sense, but only a manner of speaking. When you say that falling stones always obey the law of gravitation, is not this much the same as saying that the law only means "what stones always do"?[8]

What we call "laws" are really just our expectations of how things usually happen. For example, if you catch a falling apple from a tree, you're interrupting what it would have done naturally. A law like gravity only tells

8   Lewis, *Mere Christianity*, 17.

part of the story—there may be many other factors that cause an outcome to differ from what we expect. Every law or theory we have today is based on observation, not absolute certainty. In reality, nothing is being created or destroyed—just understood, piece by piece.

However, these things can't exist on their own. Every law needs a legislator, including the laws observed in nature. Every time something new is discovered or observed by science, it isn't an explanation against God. It's just another thing that requires God in order to be fully explained.

Sir Issac Newton isn't credited with creating gravity, just as Einstein didn't create energy, and Henry Ford didn't create the laws of combustion. These are real forces that exist—and had existed—prior to their discovery. For example, ancient humans believed God caused lightning when he was angry. But once we discovered that lightning is actually electrostatic discharges in the atmosphere, you still can't conclude that God doesn't exist. You're adding complexity, not simplifying. You might be breaking down the elemental cause of the lightning, but you're also opening the door to questions about the electron and its behavior. With knowledge, things become more complicated and require more complex answers.

Although we're sometimes wrong or don't have every law 100 percent right, we're still observing something that *is correct*. We're approaching the truth in many of these laws, but why are they stable? Were they always constant? If this universe is random, we'd expect to see randomness in all of our laws. At the very least, we wouldn't see stability in them.

Miracles and anomalies fall under the category of things we haven't yet observed. When we make a new scientific discovery—like we did when we found that the earth was round—we don't dismiss it because it goes against what we thought to be true. We follow the evidence, see how it fits into the universe around us, and allow it to clarify what we already knew.

God of the Gaps

This is also where the "God of the Gaps" argument arises. A quick claim of the skeptic is that the Christian resorts to God as an explanation for things that science has, can, or will explain.

It's a good thing to be skeptical. As I've said, the word *miracle* is overused and takes away from the actual occurrences of note. We need to start by looking for the scientific explanation, follow the evidence where it leads, and see if there's something supernatural at play. Christians are often seen as anti-science because they claim a miracle where natural explanations are at hand.

One of the world's leading geneticists, Francis Collins, considers the arguments for whether miracles are rational. He writes, "A discussion about the miraculous quickly devolves to an argument about whether or not one is willing to consider any possibility whatsoever of the supernatural."[9]

---

9   Francis S. Collins, *The Language of God: A Scientist Presents Evidence for Belief* (Simon & Schuster UK, 2007), 51.

I'm not saying that everything is a miracle, or even that everything requires God to explain. Our science has revealed a great deal about our universe, and it'll continue to go very far in unveiling the universe's mysteries. However, at a certain point, there are things that science cannot explain—and that's where we've seen miracles.

Picture a person who has lost his car keys at night. He begins searching, realizes he can't see anything, and begins searching only under a streetlight, where he has visibility. He could search for hours and find nothing, but because he's committed to searching only where he can see, he'll never find his keys. We need to acknowledge that the answer may be outside of what we know.[10]

Why do the answers have to be aligned with the things we already know to be true? Our narrow-sightedness is what keeps a lot of scientists from making new discoveries. If you look past the current light—or open a few doors—you may find the answers to the questions you have.

Belief in the Unbelievable

Regardless of your stance at this point, we all have to acknowledge that we believe in something that is unbelievable—the biblical Creation, the Big Bang, or the materialistic view of evolution.

There either was a Creator and a miracle that brought us to where we are today, or we got here from nothing by an anomaly. From that creation, we have life that ex-

---

10   Alvin Plantinga, *Warranted Christian Belief* (Christian Classics Ethereal Library, 2000), 432.

ploded from nonlife. That life either came from nonlife by random chance, or there was a guiding force behind it. This is where I do not have enough faith to be an atheist. I have faith, but it is not blind faith.

PART 3

Creation

At this point in time, it's universally agreed that there was a beginning to the universe. Hawking, Hubble, and Einstein all believed there was a beginning and considered it one of the most—if not *the* most—important scientific discoveries of all time.

The Bible says that time, space, and matter came into existence at a specific moment, with God as the cause. The materialist believes the universe emerged from a hot, dense state, with all its energy compressed into a single speck.

Many Christians take no issue with this. Christians aren't abandoning the science of the beginning or resorting to a "God of the Gaps" argument. However, the question remains: How did the energy get there in the first place?

There would have to be a belief in something eternal, regardless of your worldview. The Christian believes in an eternal God who created and used energy to bring about the universe. The materialist believes in eternal, mindless energy that coincidentally exploded into the known universe.

We could spend the next thousand years learning more about how the universe came to be. For the Christian, that just reveals more about how God works. Christians don't arbitrarily place God at the beginning because we want Him to be there—but because we logically conclude that a Designer orchestrated Creation.

What Created God?

This line of reasoning also eliminates the objection, "What created God?"

The objection implies that God is inside time, space, and matter. But for something to be made of time, space, and matter, something outside is required to be its cause. Time itself cannot create space or matter, just as matter cannot exist without space or time. The three are dependent on each other. They have a logical requirement to come into existence at the same time, with something outside as their cause.

One of the most important statements here from the perspective of philosophical theology is that God did not create "in time" but "with time." St. Augustine had a remarkable insight, which is that it is meaningless to speak about "times before creation." This is because if time is passing, then something created is *already* in existence, namely changing things and time itself, meaning that all times must be times *after* creation.[11] So if time itself is part of creation, the question about what God was doing before creation is meaningless.

This is where the objection to the immaterial arises. People claim they can't believe in something they can't see or something immaterial.

Physicality is not a prerequisite for existence. What about gravity or energy? What are these things? Nobody knows exactly what they are. However, we know they exist by the impact they have on the world around us. The laws of logic and mathematics apply the same way. Mathematics itself does not create; it simply observes something that already exists—or how things operate. Logic states something that is true, even in the absence of the given thing.

C. S. Lewis said, "I believe the sun has risen not only because I see it but because by it I see everything else."[12]

Imagine trying to look directly at the sun to learn about it. You can't do it. It will burn out your retinas, ruining your capacity to take it in. A far better way to learn about the existence, power, and quality of the sun is to look at the world it shows you, to recognize how it sustains everything you see and enables you to see it.

Our observations are what show things to be true. If we look directly at the material, we see how things are explained through science. But when we include the im-

11   Stephen M. Barr, "St. Augustine and the Beginning of Time," *Society of Catholic Scientists*, January 30, 2020, https://catholicscientists. org/articles/st-augustine-beginning-of-time/.

12   "Reflections: Christianity Makes Sense of the World," C. S. Lewis Institute, December 2013, https://www.cslewisinstitute.org/resources/ reflections-december-2013/.

material, we see the complex beauty of the world around us—beauty that requires something more.

Can Happen and Will Happen

Atheists often try to explain the origin of the universe by saying that because a law like gravity exists, something—and eventually everything—*could* come into being. But the problem is, just because something could happen doesn't mean it will happen.

Our knowledge is constantly evolving. Some might say, "Doesn't that just mean we're getting closer to the answer?" Not even close. Each new discovery only reveals deeper layers of complexity. What we thought we understood becomes even more mysterious. The goalposts keep moving, often faster than we can keep up with.

All science is conducted by humans—and that means human error or bias is inevitable. Many atheist scientists begin with a presupposition they aim to confirm. In other words, they use their worldview to prove their worldview. It's circular reasoning. You can't prove evolution by assuming evolution is true. Data are at the mercy of the interpreter, and studies can be shaped to tell the story the interpreter wants to tell.

Take a simple example: When we're tired or hungry, we sleep or eat to satisfy the need. How do we know these actions will help?

1. We understand that food contains nutrients our bodies break down to create energy.
2. We've experienced it: We eat or sleep—and we feel better.

But people didn't start eating *after* we discovered the science behind nutrition. We started eating because we knew it worked. If tomorrow we found out that we were wrong about the technicalities of digestion, would we stop eating altogether? Of course not—we'd continue just the same.

Science is a powerful tool for uncovering how things work, but being wrong about the mechanics doesn't mean the entire machine is wrong. Science is simply trying to understand the mechanisms by which our universe was created. But those mechanisms don't make the cause and effect true—they only help explain how we get from the cause to the effect.

The Value of Science

We continue to pursue science because it's a wonderful and beautiful way to uncover the mysteries of our universe. The advancements humankind has made are truly astounding, and with each step forward, we discover that everything is far more intricate than we once imagined.

Our simple explanations are often replaced with deeper questions—like the lightning example mentioned earlier. This applies to all things. Even our very existence is unexpected. The probability of the universe existing in the precise way it does is incomprehensibly low. We find that the universe is finely tuned—not only to produce everything we see but to allow life itself. That level of precision is too delicate to chalk up to random chance.

A common objection is that of course we see fine-tuning—or we wouldn't be here. But the question remains:

Why are we here rather than not here? Why is there something instead of nothing?

Can you grasp how improbable it is for a world like ours to exist if absolutely nothing existed beforehand? We can theorize that anything is possible and suggest, as naturalism does, that everything somehow came from nothing. But even if that's theoretically possible, we must ask, "Is it reasonable?"

Fine-Tuning

The fine-tuning of the universe is either an illusion or fact. But most agree: At the very least, the universe appears *to be fine-tuned.*

Agnostic physicist Paul Davies acknowledges, "Everyone agrees that the universe looks as if it was designed for life."[13]

Oxford philosopher John Leslie concurs: "It looks as if our universe is spectacularly 'fine-tuned for life.'…Small changes in this universe's basic features would have made life's evolution impossible."[14]

Theoretical physicist Stephen Hawking said the laws of physics "appear fine-tuned in the sense that if they were altered by only modest amounts, the universe would be qualitatively different, and in many cases unsuitable for the development of life…. The emergence of the com-

---

13   J. Warner Wallace, "The Inexplicable Fine-Tuning of the Foundational Forces in Our Universe," *Cold-Case Christianity*, March 21, 2025, https://coldcasechristianity.com/writings/the-inexplicable-fine-tuning-of-the-foundational-forces-in-our-universe/.

14   Ibid.

plex structures capable of supporting intelligent observers seems to be very fragile. The laws of nature form a system that is extremely fine-tuned, and very little in physical law can be altered without destroying the possibility of the development of life as we know it. Were it not for a series of startling coincidences in the precise details of physical law, it seems, humans and similar life-forms would never have come into being."[15]

There's a reason even atheist and agnostic scientists affirm this—because the precision required is undeniable. Constants like the mass of the electron, the speed of light, the strength of gravity, and the cosmological constant are so exact that any slight variation would render the universe unrecognizable—or prevent it from existing altogether.

Astrophysicist Hugh Ross offers the following analogy:

Imagine covering the entire North American continent in dimes and stacking them until they reached the moon. Now imagine stacking just as many dimes again on another billion continents the same size as North America. If you marked one of those dimes and hid it in the billions of piles you've assembled, the odds of a blindfolded friend picking out the correct dime is approximately 1 in 10^{37}, the same level of precision required in the strong nuclear force and the expansion rate of the universe.[16]

---

15   Ibid.

16   Ibid.

Philosopher Robin Collins describes it this way:

> Imagine stretching a measuring tape across the entire known universe. Now imagine one particular mark on the tape represents the correct degree of gravitational force required to create the universe we have. If this mark were moved more than an inch from where it is (on a measuring tape spanning the entire universe), the altered gravitational force would prevent our universe from coming into existence.[17]

And that's just one constant.

These numbers are humbling, to say the least. Just one of these constants would make our universe improbable. But scientists now use roughly thirty known constants to describe our universe. Taken together, the probability of all of them aligning in such a life-permitting way has been estimated to be around 1 in 10^{229}.[18]

That is more than enough evidence to warrant faith in a Creator, even though we have never seen Him.

---

17 Ibid.

18 Don Page, "Our Improbable Existence Is No Evidence for a Multiverse," *Scientific American*, August 2019, https://www.scientificamerican.com/article/our-improbable-existence-is-no-evidence-for-a-multiverse/.

PART 4

Evolution and Life

Now that we've examined the creation of the universe, the idea of a guiding force behind it no longer seems far-fetched. In fact, when we consider the extraordinary precision of the physical constants that govern our world, the notion of a God who created it all becomes not only plausible—but compelling. It's much harder to believe that such intricate design could arise from random chance.

With that in mind, let's move on to the next step of how we got to where we are today: the development of life.

Even if we grant the assumption that a random universe somehow produced the necessary conditions for life, we're still left with a major obstacle: How did life come from nonlife?

This section isn't a debate about evolution. While micro- and macroevolution—and their compatibility with Scripture—are worth discussing, they're not central to the question of God's existence. God's existence *does not hinge* on your stance about evolution.

Christians may differ on the age of the earth, the interpretation of Genesis, or the mechanisms of evolution. No matter your stance, one truth remains: Life doesn't arise from nothing without direction. However it unfolded, it points to a guiding force.

Life from Nonlife

Life as we know it can't come from nonlife without outside intervention. Just as with the creation of the universe, there must be an actualizer—something that initiates development. *Abiogenesis,* the leading naturalistic theory for the origin of life, involves a number of assumptions.

In essence, abiogenesis proposes that simple organic molecules spontaneously formed from inorganic matter and eventually learned to replicate, becoming the early ancestors of all living matter. But this raises the obvious question: How could inorganic matter spontaneously generate even the most basic organic compounds?

Again, we confront the issue that there's no such thing as a truly "simple" organic molecule. The deeper we explore molecular biology, the more complexity we uncover. We're not getting closer to a straightforward explanation for life's origin. We're discovering how staggeringly intricate—and complicated—it really is.

Furthermore, even if one organic molecule did manage to form, what are the odds it would also be capable of replication? The probability of a single life-permitting organic molecule arising from inorganic matter is vanishingly small—perhaps even impossible. But that's only the first hurdle. For life to continue, that molecule would also need to replicate successfully. How many failed organic combinations would it take before just one got it right? My guess: 4.5 billion years' worth wouldn't be enough.

I'm not a biologist—and I won't pretend to be—but let's think logically for a moment.

Complexity of Life

The functions of our bodies—and even of a single cell—are deeply interdependent. That alone raises serious questions. Consider what would be required for even the simplest organism to form from inorganic matter, survive, know it needed to reproduce, figure out how to reproduce, adapt, evolve, for some reason separate into male and female forms (not strategic), continue to survive, and eventually give rise to the complexity we see today.

For that to happen by chance defies reason. A new organism trying to survive without any need to do so is the first dilemma. Christians also believe that life came from nonlife, but we believe it came from an intelligent, intentional source. The probability of life emerging by random chance—without direction—is not just low; it's implausible. And one of the biggest challenges is time.

Even if life did emerge on its own, it would have no reason to keep living, no drive to reproduce, and certainly no logic for developing something as complex and inefficient as sexual reproduction.

This point may sound simplistic, but it raises valid questions. Why would early life forms evolve to reproduce sexually—splitting into male and female forms—when asexual reproduction would have been simpler and more efficient? Without intentional guidance, such a shift raises significant questions. The naturalist view requires too many convenient assumptions and leaves too many unanswered questions to be persuasive.

In fact, time is the greatest inhibitor to the naturalist view of evolution. The more time passes, the more things decay. Time disrupts order; it doesn't create it. Time doesn't support a theory that depends on unguided natural processes to create increasing complexity; it works against it.

Chaos and Order

Nature doesn't build—it breaks down. If humans never existed, would we expect erosion to someday carve Mount Rushmore? Would we expect volcanic eruptions to assemble the Golden Gate Bridge? A naturalist might say, "Sure—given enough time." But that actually makes the problem worse.

Hard as it is to imagine, the spontaneous appearance of Mount Rushmore or the Golden Gate Bridge would be more likely than the spontaneous emergence of human life.

Look at it this way.

Imagine dumping a puzzle out of a helicopter from ten feet up. The pieces scatter. Do they fall into place, forming the image on the box? Of course not.

Now let us take the atheist's argument of giving it more time. Imagine doing the same thing from thirty thousand feet—the pieces are scattered miles apart from each other. Time and distance don't help. They only introduce more chaos.

The same is true of life. Time doesn't organize chaos into complexity. Life doesn't emerge from nonlife. And even if it did, random mutations don't create more advanced beings. They typically degrade or distort existing functions—unless there's a guiding intelligence. A being that knew how the puzzle could fit together.

It's like code in a video game. No one looked at *Tetris* and assumed it assembled itself. No, we recognize design. We see intelligence behind the formation and know that there was a creator.

Now imagine trying to get from *Tetris* to *Mario Kart* by randomly changing a few 1s and 0s in the code. You wouldn't get a better game—you'd get a broken one.

Mutations don't innovate. Programmers do.

If we're willing to be honest—and not irrationally allergic to the idea of a Creator—it becomes clear: Systems this complex require intelligence. A game needs a programmer. Life needs a Designer.

As long as you are not unreasonably against the idea of a Creator, you can see that a game as simple as *Tetris* could never come by chance—let alone the idea that DNA and life came randomly from inorganic matter.

Nature-Made or Mind-Made

We've all looked up at the sky and seen clouds that resemble animals or shapes. But usually, the shapes are vague—our minds fill in the details more than the clouds actually form them.

Now, what if we looked up and saw *"Will you marry me?"* written in the sky? Anyone in their right mind would realize that someone paid a skywriter to fly a plane in the air and write out that message. Why? Because we know the difference between chance and choice—between random patterns and messages with a mind behind them.

If something as simple as a four-word question requires a mind, what about the longest "word" ever discovered—DNA, the three-billion-letter genetic code within every one of us?

> We now understand that DNA is an information-bearing macromolecule. The human genome is written in a chemical alphabet consisting of just four letters; it is over 3 billion letters long and carries the genetic code. It is, in that sense, the longest "word" ever discovered. If a printed, meaningful menu cannot be generated by mindless natural processes but needs the input of a mind, what are we to say about the human genome?[19]

Atheists often lean on the concept of infinity. If there's infinite time and space, then—given enough particles and energy—*anything* becomes possible. Maybe so, in theory. But it's far from reasonable. The precision of our universe's constants makes random origin virtually impossible. If any of them were off by even a fraction, the

---

19 Lennox, *Can Science Explain Everything?* 50.

universe would have collapsed, no galaxies would have formed, and life could never exist.

Listen, I may not have it all right. Maybe I misstate a few points of the materialist or naturalist view. But none of that changes the bigger truth: The more we learn, the more complexity we uncover, and the more obvious it becomes that the creation of this universe was guided by intelligence.

You may place your confidence in the idea that everything came from nothing. But the evidence for that view is far weaker than the evidence we have for the existence of Jesus Christ.

We know the universe exists. We know life exists. And between miracles and molecules, it takes a lot more faith to believe that it all happened by accident.

PART 5

Did Jesus Exist?

Up to this point, I haven't made any profound claims. I've simply shown that the so-called side of reason and logic isn't always as reasonable or logical as it appears. Compared to the materialist and naturalist claims, creationism isn't far-fetched at all.

You might say, "Okay, so there could be a god. But who's to say it's the God of Christianity?"

That is a great question.

This section isn't about proving that Jesus is the Son of God or even that the Bible is true. Right now, we're simply focusing on this: *There was a man named Jesus*. And He had a massive impact on the world.

This, like the consensus that the universe had a beginning, is not controversial stuff. The majority of intellectually honest historians agree: Jesus of Nazareth existed and was crucified by the Romans.

Now, it is true that our most comprehensive evidence comes from the Bible—specifically four eyewitness testimonies. But we're not even going there yet. Because many atheists reject the Bible as a trustworthy source, let's start with what we know about Jesus without using Christian texts.

Extra-Biblical Sources of Jesus

So, what extra-biblical sources support the claim that Jesus was a real historical figure? We have quite a few—from Roman, Jewish, secular, and even pagan sources. Many of these accounts are hostile or critical of Christianity, which actually strengthens their credibility. These aren't friendly endorsements—they're reluctant acknowledgments.

Just to name a few: Thallus, Tacitus, Mara bar Serapion, Phlegon, Pliny the Younger, Suetonius, Lucian of Samosata, Celsus, Josephus, the Jewish Talmud, and the *Toledot Yeshu*.

If we compiled what these non-Christian sources say about Jesus, we'd learn the following:

> 1) Jesus lived during the time of Tiberius Caesar. 2) He lived a virtuous life. 3) He was a wonder-worker. 4) He had a brother named James. 5) He was acclaimed to be the messiah. 6) He was crucified under Pontius Pilate. 7) He was crucified on the eve of the Jewish Passover. 8) Darkness and an earthquake occurred when he died. 9) His disciples believed he rose from the dead. 10) His disciples were willing to die for their belief. 11) Christianity spread rapidly as far as Rome.

12) His disciples denied the Roman gods and worshiped Jesus as God.[20]

Even without opening the Bible, the historical footprint of Jesus is undeniable.

The Spread of Christianity

The historical authenticity of Jesus is also evident in the impact He's had on the world—to this day. We'll address common objections—like the resurrection—soon. But first, let's look at what we can already observe.

Today, more than 30 percent of the global population identifies as Christian. That's more than two billion people following a man who was born in a small town, ministered publicly for just three years, and was executed by crucifixion.

Historical figures don't shape the world like that—unless their movement was spread through war or political power. That's how many major religions gained momentum. But not Christianity.

What about the Crusades? Yes, they were violent, but they occurred more than a thousand years after Jesus's earthly ministry—and Jesus Himself never endorsed violence. The gospel of Jesus Christ was shared and spread across the world peacefully throughout Europe, Africa, Asia, and the Middle East. The Crusades were largely about reclaiming formerly Christian lands under the au-

---

20   Frank Turek, *I Don't Have Enough Faith to Be an Atheist* (Crossway, 2004), 223.

thority of the Catholic Church—not about forced conversions in line with Christ's teaching.

Ultimately, Christianity spread across the globe because people believed in a man named Jesus—and believed what was said about Him. Many of the claims surrounding Jesus could have been easily disproven in their day, which would have killed the movement early. But that didn't happen. Why? Because the claims held up. They weren't easily refuted.

Even Bart Ehrman, an atheist historian, acknowledges this fact:

> I don't think there's any serious historian who doubts the existence of Jesus.... We have more evidence for Jesus than we have for almost anybody from his time period.[21]

Denial of Jesus as a historical figure is a fringe theory. Some atheists have gone so far in their rejection of God that they reject overwhelming historical evidence, too. You can question the Bible's accuracy or dispute the resurrection, but denying that Jesus existed at all is simply not reasonable.

---

21   Bart Ehrman, "Did Jesus Exist?" in an interview by The Infidel Guy, YouTube, https://www.youtube.com/watch?v=zdqJyk-dtLs.

PART 6

Is the Bible Accurate or Fake?

By this point, I hope you're at least open to hearing my claims about the Bible. If I'd started with this section, most 1s and 2s probably wouldn't have even made it to the second page.

That's why I began by addressing the common objections—the things that usually turn people off the moment they hear the word *Bible*. My goal is to help you keep an open mind. The Bible is dismissed far too quickly, and I believe it deserves a fair hearing.

Many assume corruption and inaccuracy with regard to the Bible. If you're a skeptic, I'd bet several talking points came to mind as soon as you read the title of this chapter. Maybe something like the following:

- "The Bible is mistranslated."

- "It's just a fairy tale—like *The Odyssey*."
- "It's a good story, but none of it actually happened."
- "We don't even know what the original said."
- "It was written too long after the events to be relevant."

Do you assume that the Bible has been corrupted over time? That because we do not have the originals, somehow that means we don't have an accurate version? Translation ruins the message?

Why take those statements as truth? Why not start with the assumption that the Bible is reliable?

I understand *why* you may not start with that assumption—it's probably because someone told you not to. A professor, a podcast, a social media post. It's confirmation bias, like anything else. If we don't like what a book says, it's easier to dismiss the whole thing than to wrestle with it. But most people never study the evidence from both sides. They hear attacks against the Bible, think they sound smart, and then roll with it.

That's been my point all along: We carry deep-seated beliefs—preloaded assumptions—without ever really testing them.

And no, I'm not judging you for having bias. Christians have bias, too. That's why, if you're a 2 or 3 and you value reason, it's worth digging deeper—looking into the historical evidence so you can come to your own educated conclusion.

No Original Copies

Let us start with the claim, "If we don't have the originals, then the Bible can't be considered historically accurate."

The assumption here is that we have no way of knowing what the original Christian message was—and therefore can't be sure what was actually written.

> There are nearly 6,000 partial or complete manuscripts of the New Testament in the original Greek language that have been catalogued, and over 18,000 in early translations into Latin, Syriac, Coptic, Arabic, and other languages. Added to this, there are thousands of quotations of the New Testament by the early Church Fathers, who wrote between the 2nd and 4th centuries. If, then, we lost *all* the New Testament manuscripts, from these quotations alone we could reconstruct a large proportion of the New Testament …
>
> By contrast … the ancient secular work with the most documentary support is Homer's *Iliad* (written around 800 BC), of which there are over 1,900 manuscript copies, dating from around 415 BC…. The earliest surviving manuscript is around 400 years.[22]

These New Testament manuscripts are old. Some date back to around AD 200, and some scholars argue we have fragments from as early as AD 125. The originals likely

---

22   Lennox, *Can Science Explain Everything?* 84–85.

date prior to AD 70. Most of what we have are copies of copies—maybe two steps removed from the original texts.

At first glance, that might sound like a weakness. "See? We don't have the originals." But in reality, this works in Christianity's favor.

If someone were trying to corrupt a sacred text, the easiest strategy would be to alter the *original*, change it, and then wave it around while saying that all the other copies refute what the original says. But we don't have just one authoritative copy—we have thousands of ancient manuscripts from all over the world. And there's security knowing that all these old copies are consistent. This widespread manuscript base makes forgery or distortion incredibly difficult.

In fact, the sheer number of manuscripts protects the message. If a copy were tampered with, it would be easy to detect by comparing it to the others. Instead of one vulnerable original, we have a global trail of textual consistency. That's a strength, not a liability.

This is why the discovery of the Dead Sea Scrolls is so important.[23] These ancient manuscripts—discovered

---

23 Many people consider the Dead Sea Scrolls to be the most significant archaeological find of the twentieth century. From 1947 to 1956, thousands of scroll fragments were uncovered from the caves near Qumran, located on the northwestern shore of the Dead Sea. Over the following decades, teams of scholars pieced these scrolls together to reconstruct an amazing library of texts from the third century BCE to the first century CE. See "What Are the Dead Sea Scrolls?" by Nathan Steinmeyer and Megan Sauter, *Biblical Archaeology Society*, May 22, 2025, https://www.biblicalarchaeology.org/daily/biblical-artifacts/dead-sea-scrolls/what_are_the_dead_sea_scrolls/.

relatively recently—confirm that the biblical text has remained remarkably consistent over time. We can now compare what we have today with documents that are thousands of years old and see that the message has not changed.

Ironically, if we *did* have the originals—and every copy around the world looked exactly the same—that might actually raise more red flags. A perfectly uniform text could be more easily manipulated, leaving us with no way to verify its authenticity. Instead, what we have is a wealth of ancient manuscripts, copied and preserved across different times and regions. That diversity helps ensure that the message we have today is faithful to the original.

Contradictions

Another argument is that the Bible contains contradictions. This is another slogan people often repeat without investigating further. The vast majority of these so-called contradictions are grammatical or spelling differences. Anything more substantial is rare—and always has a reasonable explanation.

If you were going to manipulate any text, how would you do it? You'd locate the originals, change what you wanted to change, and then claim that anything that contradicts the "original" is false. But when there are thousands of early copies from across the ancient world—all saying the same thing in different languages, with only minor spelling or grammar differences—you can be confident that you're looking at a faithful representation of the originals. The belief that there are major contradictions often stems from a lack of understanding of the text.

For example, the Gospels—Matthew, Mark, Luke, and John—contain many overlapping stories, yet the quotations from those stories are not identical. That's what you'd expect from genuine eyewitness accounts told from different perspectives. If the authors had "tried to get their stories straight," we'd see identical testimonies. Instead, the slight differences support their authenticity. They don't contradict each other—they confirm what happens when multiple people describe the same event from different angles.

The Bible vs. Other Historical Texts

The vast majority of historical scholars agree that we have a clear understanding of what the Bible originally said—even if they don't personally believe it to be true.

Alexander the Great was king of the ancient Greek kingdom of Macedon. Born in 356 BC, he succeeded his father (Philip II) to the throne at the age of twenty. Through most of his short life (died at 33) he with his military might created one of the largest empires of the ancient world, spreading from Greece to Egypt into India. Undefeated in battle, he is considered history's most successful military strategist. We know all this, right? But do we really? How do we know? We know through historical written documentation. The problem which few consider is the accuracy of said documentation. The surviving written accounts in possession of historians were written by men a few centuries after Alexander's death. At least we believe that's true considering the earliest of those accounts (originally written in the first century BC) are lost to history, leaving only hand written copies of copies whose earliest attestation is from the middle ages. So, the earliest proof mankind has in its possession for the existence of Alexander the Great appears nearly 1000 years after he was born! Put it another way, the oldest document mankind can physically produce which mentions Alexander the Great was hand written about 1000 years after his birth.[24]

I'm not questioning the historical existence of Alexander the Great. But if you find yourself starting to, ask yourself why. Is it because the comparison gives too much credibility to the Bible? That's exactly my point: Shifting your opinion simply because you don't like where the evidence leads is not intellectually honest.

There's no other book in history with the level of manuscript support the Bible has. Not only does this support show that Jesus existed—it also demands that we consider the accounts written about Him.

---

24 Daniel Gabriel, "Jesus & Alexander the Great," *RevDanTheMan* (blog), September 1, 2015, https://revdantheman.wordpress.com/2015/09/01/jesus-alexander-the-great/.

A Cohesive and Comprehensible Book

The Bible was written by more than forty authors across three continents over the span of two thousand years. Yet somehow it forms a cohesive story.

Even if you're still wrestling with the "copies of the copies" concern, that fact alone should give you pause. How could forty people, living in different times and places, write a unified book that makes clear, specific claims—many of which directly predicted the coming of a man, fulfilling those claims hundreds or even thousands of years later?

In his book *Science Speaks*, Professor Stoner outlines the mathematical probability of one person in the first century fulfilling just eight of the most clear and straightforward Messianic prophecies.

Josh and Sean McDowell quote Stoner in their book, *Evidence That Demands a Verdict*:

> We find that the chance that any man might have lived down to the present time and fulfilled all eight prophecies is 1 in 10^{17} (1 in 100,000,000,000,000,000).… In case you're wondering, the Mega Millions had a $1.6 billon jackpot in October 2018, and the odds of winning it were merely 1 in 302,575,350.[25]

---

25 Josh McDowell and Sean McDowell, PhD, *Evidence That Demands a Verdict: Life-Changing Truth for a Skeptical World* (Josh McDowell Ministry, 2017).

You might still argue, "I don't care. The Bible is still full of fairy tales and doesn't align with science."

The Bible is not a science book. The Bible speaks in a way that is childlike, not unintelligible.

> The Holy Spirit had no intention to teach astronomy… The Holy Spirit would rather speak childishly than unintelligibly to the humble and unlearned.[26]

If the Bible had used modern scientific terminology, no one in the ancient world would have understood it—and the message would never have spread. The Bible was written to be understandable by people who lived six thousand years ago and people who will live six thousand years from now.

The Bible speaks in what is called "phenomenological language," the "language of appearances."[27] This is why we say things like, "The sun rises." We know the sun doesn't actually rise—the earth rotates. But we still say it that way.

Why wouldn't the Bible speak in scientific terms?

1. The writers didn't know what they were talking about.
2. The goal of the Bible was not to teach science but to reveal the nature and character of God.

---

26 Christopher Graney, "Following the Science Isn't Always a Simple Matter," *Church Life Journal,* November 18, 2022, https://churchlifejournal.nd.edu/articles/following-the-science-isnt-always-a-simple-matter/.

27 Lennox, *Seven Days That Divide the World*, 27.

Standing alone, reason number one above might sound more reasonable—especially if you come to the Bible with skepticism. But when you take into account the extra-biblical evidence, the fulfillment of prophecy, and the scientific evidence for design in the universe, reason number two becomes more reasonable.

When we speak to children, don't we naturally use simpler language—words and ideas they can grasp? That's not because they're stupid but because they haven't yet gained the knowledge or experience to process complex concepts. That's not condescension; it's compassion.

In the same way, the people living during the time the Bible was written wouldn't have understood that the earth is a speck in an expanding universe, flying around a giant ball of nuclear fusion in a galaxy containing four hundred billion stars.

That was never the point of the Bible. Instead, it tells a story—often through poetry and metaphor—not through scientific terminology.

PART 7

The Resurrection

If the manuscripts support the reliability of what was originally said, then let's look at some of their claims.

Two of the most compelling examples are the conversions of James (Jesus's brother) and the apostle Paul. Both, according to Scripture and extra-biblical sources, initially denied Jesus—yet both went on to believe in Him and write significant portions of the New Testament. Why?

I won't go deep into their full stories (you'll find them in the Bible when you read it), but their conversions matter.

James was a skeptic. He grew up with Jesus and didn't believe His claims—until he had an encounter that changed everything.

Paul was a devout Jew who actively persecuted Christians, overseeing their deaths. Then he, too, had an encounter that led him to believe.

So, what happened? What did they see that was so convincing?

They saw something undeniable that led them there. Their faith was not blind but was supported by their personal observations.

If someone claimed to be God, I'd be skeptical, too—but if I saw them rise from the dead, I'd probably start listening to what they had to say.

Martyrs

Paul and James weren't followers during Jesus's ministry—they were late converts. But what about those who *had* followed Him from the beginning? Every disciple was martyred for their belief in the risen Christ. John himself survived multiple attempts before being exiled.

Psychology shows that people don't willingly die for something they know is false. Sure, people have died for misguided ideologies, but not for something they invented and knew to be a lie. If Jesus hadn't truly risen, surely at least one of the disciples would've cracked. But none did. Why? Because they had seen something compelling enough—something undeniable.

A closer look into the disciples shows that blind faith was not even in their nature.

Take Thomas, for example—known as "Doubting Thomas." He flat out said he wouldn't believe that Jesus rose unless he could stick his fingers into Jesus's wounds. He was a skeptic. He wasn't expecting Jesus to show up. Yet he became one of the many who gave their lives for what they saw.

Consider Simon Peter. When Jesus was arrested, Peter denied him three times and went into hiding. But after seeing the empty tomb—and then encountering the resurrected Jesus—he went on to die for his beliefs. Why would he go from self-preservation to bold proclamation unless something changed his reality?

These disciples had no motive to lie. No fame, no fortune. Each one faced jail, torture, or death. Also, if they knew that Christ was a lie, why would they have continued to follow the teachings? If they knew it was all false, they would've returned to Judaism—a familiar faith rooted in hope for a coming Messiah. Instead, they staked everything on what they had seen.

Consider the Watergate scandal. Key players lied—at first. But they eventually folded under pressure, exposing the truth to avoid prosecution. People may lie when they think they'll get away with it—but they won't die for a lie.

Hallucinations?

Some argue that the disciples were hallucinating. That grief or trauma triggered visions of Jesus. But this wasn't just a case of a few grieving followers claiming to see Him.

According to eyewitness accounts, Jesus appeared to many people over a span of forty days—and then stopped. If these were hallucinations, we'd expect continued sightings or inconsistencies in the record.

He also appeared to more than five hundred people at once. And while individuals can hallucinate, mass hallucinations—especially identical ones—have no scientific basis.

No group of Jews ever worshipped a human being as God. What led them to do it? Jews did not believe in divine men or individual resurrections. What changed their worldview virtually overnight? How do you account for the hundreds of eyewitnesses to the resurrection who lived on for decades and publicly maintained their testimony, eventually giving their lives for their belief?[28]

Resurrection's Significance

Here's the bottom line: Christianity spread—even apart from the Bible. If you removed every Bible in existence, the faith would still have made its way into every nation on earth. It wasn't an isolated religion. It wasn't spread by force. In fact, early Christians were the *persecuted,* not the persecutors.

The accounts recorded in the New Testament matter because they're comprehensive. By that I mean that you might question all the other stories in Scripture—especially the ones that seem far-fetched. But if Creation happened, and if Jesus rose from the dead, then everything in between is at least *possible.* Nothing else in the Bible is more miraculous than these two events.

So let's recap:

1. It is more reasonable to believe in a Creator than to believe everything coming into existence by random coincidence.

---

28 Timothy Keller, *The Reason for God: Belief in an Age of Skepticism* (Dutton, 2008), 219.

2. The intricate design of life points to intelligence and intention.
3. A historical figure named Jesus really did live.
4. Christianity lives and dies with the person of Christ.
5. If Jesus is who He said He was and did what He said He would do, the logical conclusion is that Christianity is true.

These are the foundational reasons why Christianity stands apart from other worldviews and why we abide by faith based on evidence, reason, and personal experience—not blind faith. Jesus made radical claims, and the resurrection validated them. If He rose from the dead—and if we have reasonable evidence that the Bible accurately preserves His words—then we have a trustworthy source of truth.

The facts show: A man named Jesus taught profound truths, was crucified, rose from the dead, and appeared to hundreds. Those eyewitnesses were so convinced by what they saw that they risked everything to spread the message. That's how Christianity grew—not from philosophy or politics, but from a resurrection.

Christianity doesn't stand on ideas. It stands on a person. If Jesus didn't live, die, and rise, the whole thing collapses.

And if you're still reading at this point, I hope that means you're at least *considering* what I've said.

In closing, let's talk about what may be the biggest obstacle to Christianity—Christians themselves.

It's one thing to see that Christianity has scientific and logical merit. It's another to reconcile that with Christians who don't represent Jesus well. I get it. So before you walk away, I want to offer a different lens—a fresh perspective on Christ and His people.

PART 8

The Good News

Enough arguments have been presented here to show that Christianity is not an unreasonable faith, and it does not rely on blind faith.

If nothing else, I hope I've helped you see that we don't know everything about the universe we live in—and that means there's room for deeper questions. Our understanding is constantly evolving, and there will always be unanswered mysteries or revisions to what we once thought was fact.

So, where does that leave us now?

Christianity might be true—at least, that's where the scientific, historical, and logical evidence seems to point. But it's still hard to make the move from a 1 to a 2 on the belief scale … or from a 2 to a 3. It can feel disorienting, especially if you've always been skeptical or even hostile toward faith. That's where humility enters: the ability to admit we don't know it all, to acknowledge that things may not be the way we were told, and to open ourselves to new possibilities. I hope I can offer some comfort here.

Nobody comes to believe in something they know is false. The fact that people convert to Christianity—often later in life—is evidence that something compelling must be at work.

Think about it: Nobody suddenly comes to believe in Santa Claus. No one on their deathbed has a divine revelation that Santa is, in fact, alive and well at the North Pole. If Christianity were a myth, we would see only the number of believers declining. But that's not what happens. We see thoughtful, informed people come to faith—often after wrestling with deep doubts.

Many of us grew up believing in things like Santa, the Easter Bunny, and the tooth fairy. And when we discovered those stories weren't true, we may have wondered whether Jesus fit into the same camp.

But if a thirty-year-old suddenly started believing in the tooth fairy, we'd think they were crazy. Yet when a thirty-year-old becomes a Christian, they often do so with eyes wide open—because the converts have had a compelling reason to come to the conclusion that a faith in Christ is real.

Did you feel a sense of *maturity* when you turned away from Christianity? Like you had finally broken free from something childish? You may have developed a kind of self-righteous indifference that felt liberating for a moment … but eventually, you discovered it was fleeting. The freedom didn't last. The high ground turned out to be hollow.

Christianity isn't a fairy tale—no matter how many atheists want to write it off that way. That's why people still convert to it—sometimes at great personal cost. There's real evidence here, and real hope.

Many former Christians are talked out of Christianity because they were never actually talked into it to begin with. It's easy to fall away from something you were only emotionally handed, rather than intellectually equipped to hold onto. When Christianity is only ever sentimental or cultural, it can't withstand the pressure of doubt. But if the foundation is solid, then even your questions can strengthen the structure.

> If you are on the wrong road, progress means doing an about-turn and walking back to the right road; and in that case the man who turns back soonest is the most progressive man.[29]

There's no shame in wrong turns. Even detours can become part of the journey—especially if they help you discover a better way forward. Detours are only a waste of time if they lead down the wrong path … or if you never stop to appreciate the view.

People who've either lost their faith—or never had it to begin with—often fall for the illusion of freedom. They want to be their own god. There's a kind of anxiety that comes with responsibility, and for many, religion just feels like one more voice telling them what to do. I get it. Faith does add a layer of responsibility.

---

29 Lewis, *Mere Christianity*, 36.

But when you understand the reward—true freedom and a love like no other—the decision becomes clear. It actually becomes easier to pick up your cross and follow Christ because you realize the price has already been paid. We have a secure place in a greater family and peace about the future.

You may feel "free" in your current lifestyle—but what happens if you try to change? What if you find out the life you thought was freedom was actually a trap? How easily could you walk away from it? Or would you find yourself stuck, confronting the hard truth that your "freedom" was really just slavery to this world?

No matter how far you've wandered, there are lights leading you back—and a guide who will walk with you if you ask.

Hurt by People

A lot of people begin their lives in the church—often because their parents or grandparents forced them—but later walk away. Sometimes it's because they were hurt by someone they trusted. Other times, it's because they were told something about God that didn't sit well with them. Maybe a distaste toward someone caused a distaste for God. And if you never knew the evidence or reasons for believing He exists, it may have seemed easier for you to dismiss God altogether.

If that's your story—if you were hurt by a church or someone who claimed to represent Christ—then hear this: What you experienced was a misrepresentation of Him.

Think of Beethoven. If you walk past someone absolutely butchering a song on the piano and they claim it's Beethoven, you don't blame Beethoven—you blame the person playing the wrong notes.

In the same light, we can't blame God for the actions of people who are "playing Jesus wrong." Yes, people have been deeply hurt by religion. Some have suffered mistreatment in Catholic schools, endured abuse from pastors, or faced judgment from members of a congregation in times of struggle. But Jesus never called for any of that. He shouldn't be blamed for people who misrepresent Him.

Hypocritical Christians

Christianity may be right—or not. But either way, something has to be ultimately right.

Often, Christians get labeled as hypocrites, and sometimes rightfully so. But that very hypocrisy points to something important: They are aiming for a good that is truly good. The standard they fall short of is not one they invented—it's the perfection of Christ. And when you're aiming at perfection, every shortcoming stands out.

Christians aren't pretending to be perfect; we're pursuing a good that isn't hypocritical, even if our pursuit is flawed. Even if we sometimes stumble, we have a guide who walks a perfect path, and our job is to follow Him as closely as we can.

Prolific British author, scholar, and Anglican layman C. S. Lewis put it this way:

> If Christianity is true then it ought to follow (a)
> That any Christian will be nicer than the same

person would be if he were not a Christian. *(b)* That any man who becomes a Christian will be nicer than he was before.

Just in the same way, if the advertisements of Whitesmile's toothpaste are true it ought to follow *(a)* That anyone who uses it will have better teeth than the same person would have if he did not use it. *(b)* That if anyone begins to use it his teeth will improve.[30]

The beauty is, we're not called to be perfect—we're called to trust the One who is. We are naturally incapable of being perfectly good, but the freedom of the gospel is this: We don't have to be.

We have a Redeemer who has taken our sins and our grief on His shoulders and bore them on the cross so we don't have to carry them. Christ will not force you into a relationship with Him—but when you accept Him, you'll begin to find real life and real meaning.

Christianity is not a religion—it's a personal relationship with Christ. Religion, left to itself, is divisive and corruptive. But a living faith in Christ is liberating. You might be right when you say that Christians can be hypocritical or judgmental. But Jesus isn't. He's the open door to the love so many have never truly known.

People search everywhere—through pleasure, relationships, success—trying to fill a void. The testimony of many who come to Christ late in life is that He was the one thing that finally filled it.

---

30   C. S. Lewis, *Mere Christianity*, 179.

It's hard to put this particular argument into words for someone who hasn't experienced it—because until you know Him for yourself, it's easy to confuse a broken religion with our living Savior.

The Map

The Bible is like a map.

C. S. Lewis said it like this:

> If a man has once looked at the Atlantic from the beach, and then goes and looks at a map of the Atlantic, he also will be turning from something real to something less real … a bit of coloured paper.…
>
> You have to remember … it is based on what hundreds and thousands of people have found out by sailing the real Atlantic.…
>
> While [your view] would be a single isolated glimpse, the map fits all those different experiences together.[31]

Trust the map—or you may spend your whole life trying to draw your own, only to realize too late that the original was right all along … assuming you don't get lost in the process. Our personal experiences matter deeply. But the beauty of Scripture is that it brings together thousands of stories and revelations to give us a fuller picture. It gives us something trustworthy because many have walked the path before us and found it true.

---

31 Lewis, *Mere Christianity*, 135–36.

Here's another way to look at it.

Imagine that a Christian and an atheist arrive at a trailhead. They see a map posted at the entrance. The Christian says, "Let's follow the map—it's already been charted, and it leads to the end."

The atheist replies, "I don't need the map. Give me enough time, and I'll find my own way through!"

Maybe he will. But there's no guarantee he will ever reach the destination—or find anything more meaningful along the way. He might get lost, doubling down on the wrong turns, and go further into the darkness to avoid admitting he was off track. And in the end, he may argue that he simply ran out of time.

Just because finding your own way is *possible* doesn't make it probable.

Science and human reason have tried to chart countless paths—but many of them lead to dead ends. The Bible, on the other hand, has traced a trail that leads to the other side. You can still ask questions along the way—but that's no reason to reject the map entirely.

You can do this life alone.

But you don't have to.

You can trust in something bigger than yourself.

Indestructible

Ultimately, Christianity is indestructible—it gets stronger the more you try to break it. The evidence points to a Creator. You can't deny that Jesus existed. And even if someone were to claim the Bible has been corrupted, you still can't explain the impact of Jesus's ministry or the rapid spread of Christianity throughout the world. Most of all, you can't erase the testimony of millions of broken people who have found life through faith in Christ.

If you're still arguing that "you can't prove a Creator" and trying to work your way around Jesus and the Bible, then you've missed the point. Believers and skeptics have gone back and forth on this for millennia. The truth is, you're not holding back because of a lack of evidence— you've made a choice. You're choosing to believe that life is meaningless. That you are nothing. Pointless. Worthless. That this life doesn't matter.

But it's not about proof. It's about wanting nothing to do with Jesus.

Why Evil?

You might be reading all this and thinking, "I honestly don't care about all the evidence. If God is real, why would He allow all this evil and suffering?"

What's behind that question? Maybe you've lost someone tragically. Maybe something terrible happened to you—or someone you loved. Let me begin by saying: I'm sorry. Truly. I'm sorry those things happened to you and to the people you love.

We live in a broken, sinful, wrecked world full of suffering. But we know it's broken only because we can compare it to the perfect standard that's been given to us. We know the world is evil because we recognize that good exists. We know our pain matters because we can imagine a better version of our situation. "A man does not call a line crooked unless he has some idea of a straight line."[32]

Just like cancer corrupts a healthy body or rust eats away at a strong car, evil is the distortion of something good. It's okay to ask questions. It's okay to cry out to God and wonder why. But if you ask, be ready to hear His answer. Evil doesn't disprove God.

The truth is, if we had God's power, we'd change everything. But if we had His knowledge, too, we wouldn't change a thing. Pain doesn't diminish His purpose. If someone left this world too soon—or at a time that felt unbearable to us—it doesn't make God evil. It makes Him the way out of the pain.

If God is real, then He knows every heart and every story. And He's working for the good of those who love Him. A relationship with Him doesn't mean you'll never be hurt again or that struggles will disappear. But it does mean there's purpose in the pain. We can trust that every bad thing will be redeemed—that He will not only justify what happened *to* us, but turn it into something that happened *for* us.

We get to share in the suffering of Jesus. But the only way for your suffering to have meaning … is to give it to Him.

Think of it this way: Our lives are a lot like those old connect-the-dot pages in coloring books. Every moment—good, bad, or in between—is a dot on the page. If you believe in an all-powerful God, then you believe He

---

32   Lewis, *Mere Christianity*, 45.

either caused or allowed each one. And from a shallow perspective, that might make God look like the bad guy.

But maybe we just don't see the picture yet.

Once we invite God into our perspective and ask for understanding, it's as if He assigns numbers to the scattered moments in our lives. We begin to see more clearly why God allowed the hard times in our lives. We start to recognize the overarching picture of what He was doing and how each moment tied into the next. Without God, it feels meaningless—but with Him, we have

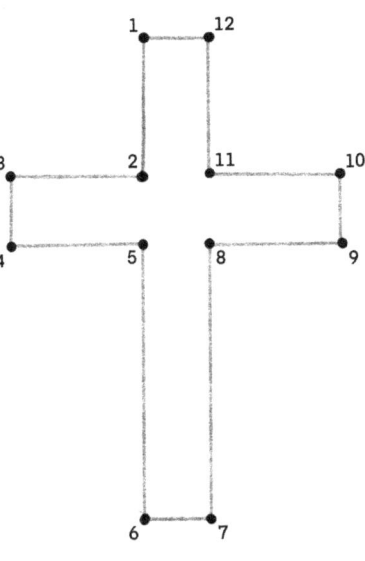

confidence, knowing that He is, in fact, doing something for our good.

A Decision

There are two sides of the fence: those who choose to believe in Jesus and those who don't. In the end, those on the right side of the fence will go with Jesus—and those on the other side will go somewhere eternally separated from Him. And if you're still sitting on the fence when that time comes, that's still a choice—and it's not a choice for Christ. Ultimately, you're deciding whether what

Jesus says sounds like someone you'd want to be with. He loves you too much to force you to be with Him.

There's a better life on the right side of the fence. Isn't it at least worth considering? Take a detour. Look for answers to the questions you may have. We're all longing for something more—we've all felt it. We try to find something and grab hold of it, only to find ourselves falling even deeper. Nothing in this world can fully satisfy.

> If I find in myself a desire which no experience in the world can satisfy, the more probable explanation is that I was made for another world … Probably earthly pleasures were never meant to satisfy it, but only to arouse it, to suggest the real thing.[33]

> We have a longing for joy, love, and beauty that no amount or quality of food, sex, friendship, or success can satisfy. We want something that nothing in this world can fulfill. Isn't that at least a clue that this "something" that we want exists? This unfulfillable longing, then, qualifies as a deep, innate human desire, and that makes it a major clue that God is there.[34]

The Best Evidence

I've spent the past few years reading and listening to some of the smartest people debate the evidence for and against

---

33 Lewis, *Mere Christianity*, 121.
34 Keller, *The Reason for God*, 135.

Creation, the Bible, and Jesus. There's so much information out there that can lead you one way or another. But the people I know with the strongest faith? They're the ones who've witnessed miracles in their own lives.

These are people who've have had experiences—personal testimonies—that anchor their belief. They don't need the first half of this book because they've already gone from broken, dead hearts to lives filled with the kind of fulfillment only Jesus can give. It's unlike anything this world can offer.

Their beliefs aren't propped up by some fleeting piece of scientific theory that might be disproven in one hundred years. Instead, they've been transformed by a relationship. If you can humble yourself enough to say, "Maybe it's true," and if you pray sincerely for a personal experience, you might just get an answer.

A self-founded relationship with Christ is the greatest proof of His existence. But unless you take that step for yourself, no amount of evidence or carefully crafted words will ever convince you that Jesus is our Savior.

The evidence I've offered may not be enough—but maybe, and hopefully—it makes you curious enough to take a step toward Jesus and to have faith in Him—not blind faith, but rather a deeply held, reasoned trust that grows and is sustained by a combination of internal conviction and external evidence.

Bibliography

Barr, Stephen M. "St. Augustine and the Beginning of Time." *Society of Catholic Scientists.* January 30, 2020. https://catholicscientists.org/articles/st-augustine-beginning-of-time/.

Collins, Francis S. *The Language of God: A Scientist Presents Evidence for Belief.* Simon & Schuster UK, 2007.

C. S. Lewis Institute. "Reflections: Christianity Makes Sense of the World." December 2013. https://www.cslewisinstitute.org/resources/reflections-december-2013/.

Ehrman, Bart. "Did Jesus Exist?" Interview by The Infidel Guy. *YouTube video*, 1:53:23. Posted March 26, 2012. https://www.youtube.com/watch?v=zdqJyk-dtLs.

Gabriel, Daniel. "Jesus & Alexander the Great." *RevDanTheMan* (blog), September 1, 2015. https://revdantheman.wordpress.com/2015/09/01/jesus-alexander-the-great/.

Graney, Christopher. "Following the Science Isn't Always a Simple Matter." *Church Life Journal*, November 18, 2022. https://churchlifejournal.nd.edu/articles/following-the-science-isnt-always-a-simple-matter/.

Keller, Timothy. *The Reason for God: Belief in an Age of Skepticism.* Dutton, 2008.

Lennox, John. *Seven Days That Divide the World: The Beginning According to Genesis and Science. 10th Anniversary Edition.* Zondervan Reflective, 2021.

Lennox, John C. *Can Science Explain Everything?* The Good Book Company, 2024.

Lewis, C. S. *Mere Christianity.* HarperOne, 2009.

Lewontin, Richard. "Billions and Billions of Demons." Review of *The Demon-Haunted World: Science as a Candle in the Dark*, by Carl Sagan. The New York Review of Books, January 9, 1997.

McDowell, Josh, and Sean McDowell. *Evidence That Demands a Verdict: Life-Changing Truth for a Skeptical World.* Thomas Nelson, 2017.

Page, Don. "Our Improbable Existence Is No Evidence for a Multiverse." *Scientific American*, August 2019. https://www.scientificamerican.com/article/our-improbable-existence-is-no-evidence-for-a-multiverse/.

Plantinga, Alvin. *Warranted Christian Belief.* Christian Classics Ethereal Library, 2000.

Steinmeyer, Nathan and Megan Sauter. "What Are the Dead Sea Scrolls?" *Biblical Archaeology Society.* May 22, 2025. https://www.biblicalarchaeology. org/daily/biblical-artifacts/dead-sea-scrolls/ what_are_the_dead_sea_scrolls/.

Turek, Frank and Norman L. Geisler. *I Don't Have Enough Faith to Be an Atheist.* Crossway, 2004.

Wallace, J. Warner. "The Inexplicable Fine-Tuning of the Foundational Forces in Our Universe." *Cold-Case Christianity.* March 21, 2025. https://coldcasechristianity.com/writings/the-inexplicable-fine-tuning-of-the-foundational-forces-in-our-universe/.

If you enjoyed this book, will you help me spread the word?

There are several ways you can help me get the word out about the message of this book . . .

- Post a 5-Star review on Amazon.
- Write about the book on your Facebook, X, Instagram, LinkedIn—any social media you regularly use!
- If you blog, consider referencing the book, or publishing an excerpt from the book with a link back to my website. You have my permission to do this as long as you provide proper credit and backlinks.
- Recommend the book—word-of-mouth is still the most effective form of advertising.
- Purchase additional copies to give away as gifts.

The best way to connect is by visiting
FaithIsntBlind.com

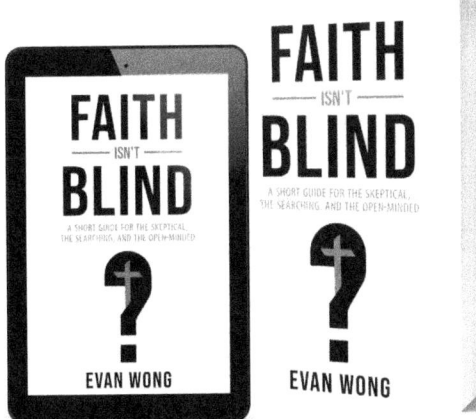

www.ingramcontent.com/pod-product-compliance
Lightning Source LLC
Chambersburg PA
CBHW071541120626
46550CB00006B/2528